SONGS of INNOCENCE

and of EXPERIENCE:

Shewing the Two Contrary States of the Human Soul

BY WILLIAM BLAKE

CONTENTS

Introduction

Piping down the valleys wild,
Piping songs of pleasant glee.
On a cloud I saw a child,
And he laughing said to me.

Pipe a song about a Lamb:
So I piped with merry cheer,
Piper pipe that song again—
So I piped, he wept to hear.

Drop thy pipe thy happy pipe
Sing thy songs of happy cheer
So I sung the same again
While he wept with joy to hear.

Piper sit thee down and write
In a book that all may read—
So he vanished from my sight,
And I plucked a hollow reed

And I made a rural pen,
And I stained the water clear,
And I wrote my happy songs,
Every child may joy to hear.

The Shepherd

How sweet is the Shepherd's sweet lot:
From the morn to the evening he strays:
He shall follow his sheep all the day
And his tongue shall be filled with
    praise.

For he hears the lambs' innocent call,
And he hears the ewes' tender reply.
He is watchful while they are in peace,
For they know when their Shepherd is
    nigh.

The Echoing Green

The sun does arise,
And make happy the skies.
The merry bells ring
To welcome the Spring.
The skylark and thrush,
The birds of the bush,
Sing louder around,
To the bells' cheerful sound,
While our sports shall be seen,
On the Echoing Green.

Old John with white hair,
Does laugh away care,
Sitting under the oak,
Among the old folk.

They laugh at our play,
And soon they all say,
Such such were the joys,
When we all girls and boys,
In our youth-time were seen,
On the Echoing Green.

Till the little ones weary
No more can be merry
The sun does descend,
And our sports have an end:
Round the laps of their mothers.
Many sisters and brothers,
Like birds in their nest,
Are ready for rest:
And sport no more seen,
On the darkening Green.

The Lamb

Little Lamb who made thee
Does thou know who made thee,
Gave thee life and bid thee feed
By the stream and o'er the mead;
Gave thee clothing of delight,
Softest clothing woolly bright;
Gave thee such a tender voice,
Making all the vales rejoice;
Little Lamb who made thee
Does thou know who made thee

Little Lamb I'll tell thee,
Little Lamb I'll tell thee;
He is called by thy name,
For he calls himself a Lamb;
He is meek and he is mild,
He became a little child:
I a child and thou a lamb.
We are called by His name.
Little Lamb God bless thee,
Little Lamb God bless thee.

The Little Black Boy

My mother bore me in the southern
    wild,
And I am black, but O! my soul is
    white.
White as an angel is the English child:
But I am black as if bereaved of light.

My mother taught me underneath a tree,
And, sitting down before the heat of
    day,
She took me on her lap and kissed me,
And, pointing to the East, began to say.

Look on the rising sun: there God does
    live
And gives His light, and gives His heat
    away,
And flowers and trees and beasts and
    men receive
Comfort in morning, joy in the noon
    day.

And we are put on earth a little space,
That we may learn to bear the beams of
  love.
And these black bodies and this
  sunburnt face
Are but a cloud, and like a shady grove.

For when our souls have learned the
  heat to bear
The cloud will vanish, we shall hear His
  voice.
Saying: come out from the grove my
  love and care,
And round my golden tent like lambs
  rejoice.

Thus did my mother say and kissed me,
And thus I say to little English boy.
When I from black, and he from white
  cloud free,
And round the tent of God like lambs
  we joy,

I'll shade him from the heat till he can
  bear
To lean in joy upon our Father's knee,
And then I'll stand and stroke his silver
  hair,
And be like him and he will then love
  me.

<u>The Blossom.</u>
Merry Merry Sparrow
Under leaves so green
A happy Blossom
Sees you swift as arrow,
Seek your cradle narrow
Near my Bosom.

Pretty Pretty Robin
Under leaves so green
A happy Blossom
Hears you sobbing sobbing
Pretty Pretty Robin
Near my Bosom.

The Chimney Sweeper

When my mother died I was very
young,
And my father sold me while yet my
tongue,
Could scarcely cry weep weep weep
weep.
So your chimneys I sweep and in soot I
sleep.

There's little Tom Dacre, who cried
when his head,
That curled like a lamb's back, was
shaved; so I said,
Hush Tom never mind it, for, when
your head's bare,
You know that the soot cannot spoil
your white hair.

And so he was quiet, and that very
night,
As Tom was a sleeping he had such a
sight,
That thousands of sweepers Dick, Joe,
Ned, and Jack,
Were all of them locked up in coffins
of black.

And by came an Angel who had a
bright key,
And he opened the coffins and set them
all free.
Then down a green plain leaping
laughing they run
And wash in a river and shine in the
Sun.

Then naked and white, all their bags
left behind,
They rise upon clouds, and sport in the
wind.
And the Angel told Tom if he'd be a
good boy,
He'd have God for his father and never
want joy.

And so Tom awoke and we rose in the
dark,
And got with our bags and our brushes
to work.
Tho' the morning was cold, Tom was
happy and warm.
So if all do their duty, they need not
fear harm.

The Little Boy Lost

Father, father, where are you going
O do not walk so fast,
Speak father, speak to your little boy
Or else I shall be lost,

The night was dark, no father was there
The child was wet with dew.
The mire was deep, and the child did
    weep
And away the vapour flew,

The Little Boy Found

The little boy lost in the lonely fen,
Led by the wandering light,
Began to cry, but God ever nigh,
Appeared like his father in white.

He kissed the child and by the hand led
And to his mother brought.
Who in sorrow pale through the lonely
    dale
Her little boy weeping sought.

Laughing Song

When the green woods laugh with the voice of joy
And the dimpling stream runs laughing by,
When the air does laugh with our merry wit,
And the green hill laughs with the noise of it.

When the meadows laugh with lively green
And the grasshopper laughs in the merry scene,
When Mary and Susan and Emily
With their sweet round mouths sing Ha, Ha, He.

When the painted birds laugh in the shade
Where our table with cherries and nuts is spread,
Come live and be merry and join with me,
To sing the sweet chorus of Ha, Ha, He.

A Cradle Song

Sweet dreams form a shade.
O'er my lovely infant's head.
Sweet dreams of pleasant streams.
By happy silent moony beams.

Sweet sleep with soft down.
Weave thy brows an infant crown.
Sweet sleep Angel mild,
Hover o'er my happy child.

Sweet smiles in the night
Hover over my delight.
Sweet smiles Mother's smiles,
All the livelong night beguiles.

Sweet moans, dovelike sighs,
Chase not slumber from thy eyes.
Sweet moans, sweeter smiles,
All the dovelike moans beguiles.

Sleep sleep happy child.
All creation slept and smiled.
Sleep sleep, happy sleep,
While o'er thee thy mother weep.

Sweet babe in thy face,
Holy image I can trace.
Sweet babe once like thee,
Thy maker lay and wept for me.

Wept for me for thee for all,
When he was an infant small.
Thou his image ever see.
Heavenly face that smiles on thee.

Smiles on thee on me on all,
Who became an infant small.
Infant smiles are his own smiles.
Heaven and earth to peace beguiles.

The Divine Image.

To Mercy Pity Peace and Love,
All pray in their distress:
And to these virtues of delight
Return their thankfulness.

For Mercy Pity Peace and Love,
Is God our father dear;
For Mercy Pity Peace and Love,
Is Man his child and care.

For Mercy has a human heart
Pity, a human face:
And Love, the human form divine.
And Peace, the human dress.

Then every man of every clime,
That prays in his distress,
Prays to the human form divine
Love Mercy Pity Peace.

And all must love the human form,
In heathen, turk, or jew.
Where Mercy, Love and Pity dwell
There God is dwelling too.

Holy Thursday

Twas on a Holy Thursday their
  innocent faces clean
The children walking two and two in
  red and blue and green
Grey headed beadles, walked before
  with wands as white as snow
Till into the high dome of Paul's they
  like Thames waters flow.

O what a multitude they seemed, these
  flowers of London town
Seated in companies they sit, with
  radiance all their own.
The hum of multitudes was there but
  multitudes of lambs
Thousands of little boys and girls
  raising their innocent hands.

Now like a mighty wind they raise to
  heaven the voice of song
Or like harmonious thunderings the
  seats of heaven among.
Beneath them sit the aged men wise
  guardians of the poor,
Then cherish pity lest you drive an
  angel from your door.

Nurse's Song

When voices of children are heard on
 the green
And laughing is heard on the hill,
My heart is at rest within my breast
And everything else is still.

Then come home, my children, the sun
 is gone down
And the dews of night arise
Come, come, leave off play, and let us
 away,
Till the morning appears in the skies.

No no, let us play, for it is yet day
And we cannot go to sleep
Besides in the sky, the little birds fly
And the hills are all covered with
 sheep.

Well well go and play till the light
 fades away
And then go home to bed
The little ones leaped and shouted and
 laughed
And all the hills echoed.

Night

The sun descending in the west.
The evening star does shine.
The birds are silent in their nest.
And I must seek for mine.
The moon like a flower.
In heaven's high bower;
With silent delight.
Sits and smiles on the night.

Farewell green fields and happy
  groves.
Where flocks have took delight;
Where lambs have nibbled, silent
  moves
The feet of angels bright;
Unseen, they pour blessing.
And joy without ceasing.
On each bud and blossom,
And each sleeping bosom.

They look in every thoughtless nest
Where birds are covered warm;
They visit caves of every beast,
To keep them all from harm:
If they see any weeping
That should have been sleeping,
They pour sleep on their head
And sit down by their bed.

When wolves and tigers howl for prey,
They pitying stand and weep;
Seeking to drive their thirst away,
And keep them from the sheep.
But if they rush dreadful,
The angels most heedful,
Receive each mild spirit,
New worlds to inherit.

And there the lion's ruddy eyes,
Shall flow with tears of gold:
And pitying the tender cries,
And walking round the fold:
Saying: wrath by his meekness
And by his health, sickness,
Is driven away,
From our immortal day.

And now beside thee bleating lamb,
I can lie down and sleep;
Or think on him who bore thy name,
Graze, after thee and weep.
For, washed in life's river,
My bright mane for ever,
Shall shine like the gold,
As I guard o'er the fold.

<u>Spring</u>

Sound the Flute!
Now it's mute.
Birds delight
Day and Night.
Nightingale
In the dale
Lark in Sky
Merrily
Merrily Merrily to welcome in the Year

Little Boy
Full of joy.

Little Girl
Sweet and small.
Cock does crow
So do you.
Merry voice
Infant noise
Merrily Merrily to welcome in the Year

Little Lamb,
Here I am.
Come and lick
My white neck.
Let me pull
Your soft Wool.
Let me kiss
Your soft face.
Merrily Merrily we welcome in the
    Year

Infant Joy

I have no name
I am but two days old.—
What shall I call thee?
I happy am
Joy is my name.—
Sweet joy befall thee!

Pretty joy!
Sweet joy but two days old,
Sweet joy I call thee:
Thou dost smile.
I sing the while
Sweet joy befall thee.

A Dream

Once a dream did weave a shade.
O'er my Angel-guarded bed.
That an Emmet lost its way
Where on grass methought I lay,

Troubled wildered and forlorn,
Dark benighted travel-worn,
Over many a tangled spray,
All heart-broke, I heard her say.

O my children! do they cry,
Do they hear their father sigh,
Now they look abroad to see,
Now return and weep for me.

Pitying, I dropped a tear:
But I saw a glow-worm near:
Who replied, What wailing wight
Calls the watchman of the night.

I am set to light the ground,
While the beetle goes his round:
Follow now the beetles hum,
Little wanderer hie thee home.

On Another's Sorrow

Can I see another's woe,
And not be in sorrow too.
Can I see another's grief,
And not seek for kind relief.

Can I see a falling tear,
And not feel my sorrow's share.
Can a father see his child,
Weep, nor be with sorrow filled.

Can a mother sit and hear,
An infant groan, an infant fear—
No no never can it be.
Never never can it be.

And can he who smiles on all
Hear the wren with sorrows small,
Hear the small bird's grief and care,
Hear the woes that infants bear—

And not sit beside the nest
Pouring pity in their breast.
And not sit the cradle near
Weeping tear on infant's tear.

And not sit both night and day,
Wiping all our tears away.
O! no never can it be.
Never never can it be.

He doth give His joy to all.
He becomes an infant small,
He becomes a man of woe
He doth feel the sorrow too.

Think not, thou canst sigh a sigh,
And thy maker is not by.
Think not, thou canst weep a tear,
And thy maker is not near.

O! he gives to us his joy.
That our grief he may destroy
Till our grief is fled and gone
He doth sit by us and moan

Introduction

Hear the voice of the Bard!
Who Present, Past, and Future sees
Whose ears have heard,
The Holy Word,
That walked among the ancient
  trees.

Calling the lapsed Soul
And weeping in the evening dew;
That might control
The starry pole;
And fallen fallen light renew!

O Earth O Earth return!
Arise from out the dewy grass;
Night is worn,
And the morn
Rises from the slumberous mass.

Turn away no more:
Why wilt thou turn away
The starry floor
The watery shore
Is given thee till the break of day

EARTH'S Answer.

Earth raised up her head.
From the darkness dread and drear.
Her light fled.
Stony dread!
And her locks covered with grey
    despair.

Prisoned on watery shore
Starry Jealousy does keep my den
Cold and hoar
Weeping o'er,
I hear the Father of the ancient men.

Selfish father of men
Cruel jealous selfish fear
Can delight
Chained in night
The virgins of youth and morning bear.

Does spring hide its joy
When buds and blossoms grow?
Does the sower?
Sow by night?
Or the ploughman in darkness plough?

Break this heavy chain
That does freeze my bones around
Selfish! vain!
Eternal bane!
That free Love with bondage bound

The CLOD and the PEBBLE

Love seeketh not Itself to please,
Nor for itself hath any care;
But for another gives, its ease.
And builds a Heaven in Hell's despair.

So sung a little Clod of Clay,
Trodden with the cattle's feet;
But a Pebble of the brook,
Warbled out these metres meet.

Love seeketh only Self to please,
To bind another to Its delight;
Joys in another's loss of ease,
And builds a Hell in Heaven's despite.

Holy Thursday

Is this a holy thing to see,
In a rich and fruitful land,.
Babes reduced to misery,
Fed with cold and usurous hand?

Is that trembling cry a song?
Can it be a song of joy?
And so many children poor?
It is a land of poverty!

And their sun does never shine,
And their fields are bleak and bare,
And their ways are filled with thorns,
It is eternal winter there.

For wherever the sun does shine,
And wherever the rain does fall;
Babe can never hunger there,
Nor poverty the mind appall.

<u>The Little Girl Lost</u>

In futurity
I prophesy
That the earth from sleep,
(Grave the sentence deep)

Shall arise and seek
For her maker meek:
And the desert wild
Become a garden mild.

In the southern clime,
Where the summer's prime
Never fades away;
Lovely Lyca lay.

Seven summers old
Lovely Lyca told.
She had wandered long
Hearing wild birds song.

Sweet sleep come to me
Underneath this tree;
Do father, mother weep.—
Where can Lyca sleep.

Lost in desert wild
Is your little child.
How can Lyca sleep,
If her mother weep.

If her heart does ache,
Then let Lyca wake.
If my mother sleep,
Lyca shall not weep.

Frowning frowning night,
O'er this desert bright,
Let thy moon arise,
While I close my eyes.

Sleeping Lyca lay;
While the beasts of prey,
Come from caverns deep,
Viewed the maid asleep.

The kingly lion stood
And the virgin viewed,
Then he gamboled round
O'er the hallowed ground.

Leopards, tigers play,
Round her as she lay;
While the lion old,
Bowed his mane of gold.

And her bosom lick,
And upon her neck,
From his eyes of flame,
Ruby tears there came;

While the lioness
Loosed her slender dress,
And naked they conveyed
To caves the sleeping maid.

The Little Girl Found

All the night in woe,
Lyca's parents go;
Over valleys deep
While the deserts weep.

Tired and woe-begone,
Hoarse with making moan,
Arm in arm seven days,
They traced the desert ways.

Seven nights they sleep
Among shadows deep:
And dream they see their child
Starved in desert wild.

Pale through pathless ways
The fancied image strays,
Famished, weeping, weak,
With hollow piteous shriek.

Rising from unrest,
The trembling woman pressed
With feet of weary woe;
She could no further go.

In his arms he bore
Her armed with sorrow sore;
Till before their way,
A couching lion lay.

Turning back was vain,
Soon his heavy mane,
Bore them to the ground;
Then he stalked around.

Smelling to his prey;
But their fears allay.
When he licks their hands;
And silent by them stands.

They look upon his eyes,
Filled with deep surprise:
And wondering behold,
A spirit armed in gold.

On his head a crown
On his shoulders down.
Flowed his golden hair,
Gone was all their care.

Follow me he said,
Weep not for the maid;
In my palace deep,
Lyca lies asleep.

Then they followed
Where the vision led,
And saw their sleeping child,
Among tigers wild.

To this day they dwell
In a lonely dell,
Nor fear the wolvish howl,
Nor the lion's growl.

THE Chimney Sweeper

A little black thing among the snow:
Crying weep, weep, in notes of woe!
Where are thy father and mother? say?
They are both gone up to the church to
 pray.

Because I was happy upon the heath,
And smiled among the winter's snow:
They clothed me in the clothes of death,
And taught me to sing the notes of woe.

And because I am happy, and dance and
 sing,.
They think they have done me no injury:
And are gone to praise God and his
 Priest and King,
Who made up a heaven of our misery.

NURSE'S Song

When the voices of children, are heard
 on the green
And whisperings are in the dale:
The days of my youth rise fresh in my
 mind,
My face turns green and pale.

Then come home my children, the sun
 is gone down
And the dews of night arise
Your spring and your day, are wasted
 in play,
And your winter and night in disguise.

The SICK ROSE

O Rose, thou art sick.
The invisible worm.
That flies in the night
In the howling storm:

Has found out thy bed
Of crimson joy:
And his dark secret love
Does thy life destroy.

THE FLY

Little Fly
Thy summer's play,
My thoughtless hand
Has brushed away.

Am not I
A fly like thee?
Or art not thou
A man like me?

For I dance
And drink and sing:
Till some blind hand
Shall brush my wing.

If thought is life
And strength and breath:
And the want
Of thought is death;

Then am I
A happy fly,
If I live,
Or if I die.

The Angel

I Dreamt a Dream! What can it mean?
And that I was a maiden Queen:
Guarded by an Angel mild:
Witless woe, was ne'er beguiled!

And I wept both night and day
And he wiped my tears away
And I wept both day and night
And hid from him my heart's delight.

So he took his wings and fled;
Then the morn blushed rosy red;
I dried my tears, and armed my fears,
With ten thousand shields and spears.

Soon my Angel came again;
I was armed, he came in vain;
For the time of youth was fled
And grey hairs were on my head

The Tiger

Tiger Tiger burning bright,
In the forests of the night:
What immortal hand or eye,
Could frame thy fearful symmetry?

In what distant deeps or skies
Burnt the fire of thine eyes!
On what wings dare he aspire?
What the hand, dare seize the fire?

And what shoulder, and what art.
Could twist the sinews of thy heart?
And, when thy heart began to beat,
What dread hand? and what dread
    feet?

What the hammer? what the chain,
In what furnace was thy brain?
What the anvil? what dread grasp,
Dare its deadly terrors clasp!

When the stars threw down their
    spears
And watered heaven with their tears:
Did he smile his work to see?
Did He who made the Lamb make
    thee

Tiger Tiger burning bright,
In the forests of the night:
What immortal hand or eye,
Dare frame thy fearful symmetry?

My Pretty ROSE TREE

A flower was offered to me;
Such a flower as May never bore,
But I said I've a Pretty Rose-tree,
And I passed the sweet flower o'er.

Then I went to my Pretty Rose-tree;
To tend her by day and by night.
But my Rose turned away with
  jealousy:
And her thorns were my only delight.

AH! SUNFLOWER

Ah, Sun-flower! weary of time,
Who countest the steps of the Sun:
Seeking after that sweet golden clime
Where the traveler's journey is done.

Where the Youth pined away with
  desire,
And the pale Virgin shrouded in snow:
Arise from their graves and aspire,
Where my Sun-flower wishes to go.

THE LILY

The modest Rose puts forth a thorn:
The humble Sheep, a threatening horn:
While the Lily white, shall in Love
  delight,
Nor a thorn nor a threat stain her
  beauty bright.

The GARDEN of LOVE

I went to the Garden of Love,
And saw what I never had seen;
A Chapel was built in the midst,
Where I used to play on the green.

And the gates of this Chapel were
  shut,
And Thou shalt not, writ over the
  door;
So I turned to the Garden of Love
That so many sweet flowers bore.

And I saw it was filled with graves,
And tombstones where flowers should
  be;
And Priests in black gowns, were
  walking their rounds,
And binding with briars, my joys and
  desires.

The Little Vagabond

Dear Mother, dear Mother, the Church
    is cold,
But the Alehouse is healthy and
    pleasant and warm.
Besides I can tell where I am used
    well,
Such usage in heaven will never do
    well.

But if at the Church they would give
    us some Ale,
And a pleasant fire our souls to regale:
We'd sing and we'd pray all the
    livelong day:
Nor ever once wish from the Church
    to stray.

Then the Parson might preach and
    drink and sing,
And we'd be as happy as birds in the
    spring;
And modest dame Lurch, who is
    always at Church,
Would not have bandy children nor
    fasting nor birch.

And God like a father rejoicing to see,
His children as pleasant and happy as
    he:
Would have no more quarrel with the
    Devil or the Barrel,
But kiss him and give him both drink
    and apparel.

LONDON

I wander through each chartered street,
Near where the chartered Thames does
  flow
A mark in every face I meet
Marks of weakness, marks of woe.

In every cry of every Man,
In every Infant's cry of fear,
In every voice; in every ban.
The mind-forged manacles I hear

How the Chimney-sweeper's cry
Every blackening Church appalls,
And the hapless Soldier's sigh
Runs in blood down Palace walls

But most through midnight streets I
  hear
How the youthful Harlot's curse
Blasts the new born Infant's tear
And blights with plagues the Marriage
  hearse

The Human Abstract.

Pity would be no more,
If we did not make somebody Poor:
And Mercy no more could be,
If all were as happy as we;

And mutual fear brings peace:
Till the selfish loves increase,
Then Cruelty knits a snare,
And spreads his baits with care.

He sits down with holy fears,
And waters the ground with tears;
Then Humility takes its root
Underneath his foot.

Soon spreads the dismal shade
Of Mystery over his head;
And the Caterpillar and Fly,
Feed on the Mystery.

And it bears the fruit of Deceit,
Ruddy and sweet to eat:
And the Raven his nest has made
In its thickest shade.

The Gods of the earth and sea,
Sought through Nature to find this
    Tree,
But their search was all in vain:
There grows one in the Human Brain.

<u>INFANT SORROW</u>

My mother groaned! my father wept.
Into the dangerous world I leapt:
Helpless, naked, piping loud:
Like a fiend hid in a cloud.

Struggling in my father's hands:
Striving against my swaddling bands:
Bound and weary I thought best
To sulk upon my mother's breast.

A Little BOY Lost

Nought loves another as itself,
Nor venerates another so,
Nor is it possible to Thought
A greater than itself to know:

And Father, how can I love you,
Or any of my brothers more?
I love you like the little bird
That picks up crumbs around the door.

The Priest sat by and heard the child,
In trembling zeal he seized his hair:
He led him by his little coat:
And all admired his Priestly care.

And standing on the altar high,
Lo what a fiend is here! said he:
One who sets reason up for judge
Of our most holy Mystery.

The weeping child could not be heard,
The weeping parents wept in vain:
They stripped him to his little shirt,
And bound him in an iron chain.

And burned him in a holy place
Where many had been burned before:
The weeping, parents wept in vain,
Are such things done on Albion's
  shore.

A Little GIRL Lost

Children of the future Age,
Reading this indignant page:
Know that in a former time,
Love! sweet Love! was thought a
  crime.

In the age of Gold,
Free from winter's cold:
Youth and maiden bright,
To the holy light,
Naked in the sunny beams delight.

Once a youthful pair,
Filled with softest care,
Met in garden bright,
Where the holy light,
Had just removed the curtains of the
  night.

There, in rising day,
On the grass they play;
Parents were afar;
Strangers came not near;
And the maiden soon forgot her fear.

Tired with kisses sweet,
They agree to meet,
When the silent sleep
Waves o'er heaven's deep;
And the weary tired wanderers weep.

To her father white
Came the maiden bright;
But his loving look,
Like the holy book,
All her tender limbs with terror shook.

Ona! pale and weak!
To thy father speak:
O the trembling fear!
O the dismal care!
That shakes the blossoms of my hoary
  hair

A POISON TREE

I was angry with my friend:
I told my wrath, my wrath did end.
I was angry with my foe:
I told it not, my wrath did grow.

And I watered it in fears,
Night and morning with my tears:
And I sunned it with smiles,
And with soft deceitful wiles.

And it grew both day and night,
Till it bore an apple bright.
And my foe beheld it shine,
And he knew that it was mine.

And into my garden stole,
When the night had veiled the pole
In the morning glad I see,
My foe outstretched beneath the tree.

To Tirzah

Whatever is Born of Mortal Birth.
Must be consumed with the Earth
To rise from Generation free;
Then what have I to do with thee?

The Sexes sprung from Shame and
  Pride
Blowed in the morn; in evening died
But Mercy changed Death into Sleep;
The Sexes rose to work and weep.

Thou Mother of my Mortal part,
With cruelty didst mold my Heart;
And with false-self-deceiving tears,
Didst bind my Nostrils Eyes and Ears.

Didst close my Tongue in senseless
  clay
And me to Mortal Life betray:
The Death of Jesus set me free,
Then what have I to do with thee?

The School Boy

I love to rise in a summer morn,
When the birds sing on every tree;
The distant huntsman winds his horn,
And the skylark sings with me.
O! what sweet company.

But to go to school in a summer morn,
O! it drives all joy away:
Under a cruel eye outworn.
The little ones spend the day.
In sighing and dismay.

Ah! then at times I drooping sit,
And spend many an anxious hour.
Nor in my book can I take delight,
Nor sit in learning's bower,
Worn through with the dreary shower.

How can the bird that is born for joy,
Sit in a cage and sing.
How can a child when fears annoy,
But droop his tender wing,
And forget his youthful spring.

O! father and mother, if buds are nipped,
And blossoms blown away,
And if the tender plants are stripped
Of their joy in the springing day,
By sorrow and care's dismay.

How shall the summer arise in joy,
Or the summer fruits appear,
Or how shall we gather what griefs destroy,
Or bless the mellowing year,
When the blasts of winter appear.

<u>The Voice Of The Ancient Bard</u>

Youth of delight come hither.
And see the opening morn.
Image of truth new born.
Doubt is fled and clouds of reason.
Dark disputes and artful teasing.
Folly is an endless maze,
Tangled roots perplex, her ways,
How many have fallen there!
They stumble all night over bones of the dead;
And feel they know not what but care;
And wish to lead others when they should be led.

CPSIA information can be obtained
at www.ICGtesting.com
Printed in the USA
LVHW091007030720
659164LV00013BA/412